Similar

Between

Hinduism

&

Islam

Similarities
Between
Hinduism
&
Islam

Dr. Zakir Naik

Islamic Book Service

SIMILARITIES BETWEEN HINDUISM & ISLAM
By: Dr. Zakir Naik

ISBN 81-7231-935-5

First Edition : 2008
Reprint Edition : 2011

Published by

Islamic Book Service (P) Ltd.

2872-74, Kucha Chelan, Darya Ganj,
New Delhi-110002 **(India)**
Ph.: 011-23244556, 23253514, 23272893, 23286551
Fax: 011-23247899, 23277913
E-mail: islamic@eth.net
Website: www.islamicbookservice.co / www.islamicbookservice.asia

Our Associates:

♦ Al-Munna Book Shop Ltd. **(U.A.E.)**
   (Sharjah) *Tel.:* 06-561-5483, 06-561-4650
   (Dubai) *Tel.:* 04-352-9294

♦ Azhar Academy Ltd. **London (United Kingdom)**
   Tel.: 020-8911-9797

♦ Lautan Lestari (Lestari Books), **Jakarta (Indonesia)**
   Tel.: 0062-21-35-23456

♦ Husami Book Depot, **Hyderabad (India)**
   Tel.: 040-6680-6285

Printed in India

ABOUT THE AUTHOR

A Medical Doctor by professional training, Dr. Zakir Naik is Renowned as a Dynamic International orator on Islam and Comparative Religion, Dr. Zakir clarifies Islamic view points and clears Misconception about Islam using the Qur'an and authentic Ahadeeth and other Religious scriptures as a basis, in conjunction with Reason, Logic and Scientific facts. He is popular for his critical analysis and convincing answer to challenging Questions. In the last 6 years he has delivered more than 600 Public Talks in India, U.S.A., Canada, U.K., Australia, Saudi Arabia, U.A.E., Kuwait, Qatar, Bahrain, Singapore, Malaysia and many other countries.

Sheikh Ahmad Deedat, the world famous orator on Islam and Comparative Religion, who had called Dr. Zakir "Deedat Plus" in 1994, presented a plaque in May 2000 with engraving "Awarded to Zakir Abdul Karim Naik for his achievement in the field of Da'wah and the studies of comparative religion. Son what you have done in 4 years had taken me 40 years to accomplish, Alhamdulillah."

Dr. Zakir has also authored several books on Islam and Comparative Religion namely, *Qur'an & Modern Science - Conflict or Conciliation, Answers to Non Muslim's Common Questions About Islam* etc.

Note : PBUH — Peace Be upon Him
Swt — Subhanahu we Ta'ala

v

CONTENTS

INTRODUCTION

In this book we shall seek to find similarities or common ground between two major religions of the world: *Hinduism* and *Islam*. The approach adopted in this work is based on the following Verse of the Glorious Qur'an : Surah Al Imran Chapter 3 Verse 64,

> Say "O People Of the Book!
> Come to common terms
> As between us and you:
> That we worship none but Allah;
> That we associate no partners with Him;
> That we erect not, From among ourselves,
> Lords and patrons other than Allah."
> If then they turn back,
> Say ye: "Bear witness That we (at least)
> Are Muslims (submitting To Allah's Will)."

We shall focus on how one should try to have a correct understanding of a religion and also provide a brief introduction to Islam and Hinduism.

1

CORRECT UNDERSTANDING OF A RELIGION

a. Don't observe followers of a Religion. Refer to Authentic Sources of that Religion.

Followers of major religions, whether it be Hinduism, Islam or Christianity, have divided themselves and their beliefs into various sects.

It is not appropriate for one to try to understand a religion by observing the followers of that religion. Most followers may themselves not be aware of the correct teachings of their religion. Thus, the best and the most appropriate method of understanding any religion is to understand the authentic sources of that religion, i.e. the sacred scriptures of that religion.

b. Authentic Sources of Islam.

Allah (swt), Almighty God, says in the Glorious Qur'an: Surah Al Imran Chapter 3 Verse 103,

And hold fast, All together,
by the Rope Which Allah (stretches out for you),
and be not divided among yourselves.

The "rope of Allah refers" to the Glorious Qur'an. Allah (swt) says that Muslims should not be divided and that the only unifying factor is the authentic source of the religion of Islam i.e. the Glorious Qur'an. Allah (swt) also says in the Glorious Qur'an in several places including (Al

3

Qur'an: Surah Nissa Chapter 4 Verse 59) "O *ye who believe! Obey Allah, and obey the Messenger....*"

To understand the Qur'an better we have to refer to the explanation of the Qur'an by Prophet Muhammad (PBUH) on whom the Qur'an was revealed. Thus the best and the most appropriate method of understanding Islam is to understand the authentic sources of Islam which are the Glorious Qur'an, (the words of Almighty Allah) and the authentic *Ahadith*, (i.e. the sayings and traditions of Prophet Muhammad (PBUH).

c.   Authentic Sources of Hinduism.

Similarly, the best and the most appropriate method of understanding Hinduism is to understand the authentic sources i.e. the sacred scriptures of Hinduism. The most sacred and authentic Scriptures of Hinduism are the Vedas, followed by the Upanishads, the Itihaas, Bhagvad Gita, Puranas, etc.

Let us understand these two major religions of the world, i.e. Islam and Hinduism, by studying and analyzing the authentic Scriptures of these two major religions of the world.

d.   Emphasis on those Similarities, which are not commonly known.

In this work on '*Similarities between Islam and Hinduism*', we shall not lay emphasis on those similarities which are known by almost all the followers of both the religions e.g. a person should always speak the truth, he should not lie, he should not steal, he should be kind, he should not be cruel, etc. Instead, we shall consider those similarities, which are not commonly known by all the followers and hence are known only to those who are familiar with the contents of their sacred Scriptures.

4

2

INTRODUCTION OF ISLAM

1. Definition of Islam.

Islam is an Arabic word, which comes from the word *'Salm'* which means peace and from *'Silm'*, which means *submitting your will to Allah - the Almighty God*. In short Islam means peace acquired by submitting your will to Allah (swt).

The word Islam is mentioned in several places in the Qur'an and the *Hadith* including Surah Al Imran, Chapter 3, Verse 19 and Verse 85.

2. Definition of a Muslim.

A Muslim is a person who submits his will to Allah - the Almighty God. The word Muslim is mentioned several times in the Qur'an and *Hadith* including Surah Al Imran Chapter 3 Verse 64 and Surah Fussilat Chapter 41 Verse 33.

3. A misconception about Islam.

Many people have a misconception that Islam is a new religion that was formulated 1400 years ago, and that Prophet Muhammad (PBUH) was the founder of Islam. However, let me clarify that Islam is not the name of some unique religion presented for the first time by Prophet Muhammad (PBUH) who should, on that account, be called the founder of Islam.

The Qur'an states that Islam - the complete submission of man before his one and only Unique Creator - is the one and only faith and way of life consistently revealed by God to humankind from the very beginning. Noah, Solomon, David, Abraham, Isaac, Moses, and Jesus (peace be upon them all) - prophets who appeared at different times and places - all propagated the same faith and conveyed the same message of *Tawheed* (Oneness of God), *Risaalat* (Prophethood) and *Aakhirah* (the Hereafter). These prophets of God were not founders of different religions to be named after them. They were each reiterating the message and faith of their predecessors.

However, Muhammad (PBUH) was the last Prophet of God. God revived through him the same genuine faith, which had been conveyed by all His Prophets. This original message was earlier corrupted and split into various religions by people of different ages, who indulged in interpolations and admixture. These alien elements were eliminated by God, and Islam - in its pure and original form - was transmitted to humankind through Prophet Muhammad (PBUH).

Since there was to be no messenger after Muhammad (PBUH), the Book revealed to him (i.e. the Glorious Qur'an) was preserved word by word so that it should be a source of guidance for all times. Thus the religion of all the prophets was *'total submission to God's will'* and one word for that in the Arabic language is *'Islam'*. Abraham and Jesus (peace be upon them) too were Muslims, as Allah testifies in Al-Qur'an : Surah Al Imran Chapter 3 Verse 52 and 67 respectively.

3

INTRODUCTION OF HINDUISM

1. **Definition of a Hindu.**

A. The word *'Hindu'* has geographical significance and was used originally to refer to those people who lived beyond the river Sindhu or the region watered by the river Indus.

B. Historians say that it was first used by the Persians who came to India through the North Western passes of the Himalayas. The word 'Hindu' was also used by the Arabs.

C. This word 'Hindu' is nowhere mentioned in Indian Literature or Hindu Scriptures before the advent of Muslims to India, according to the *Encyclopedia of Religions and Ethics 6:690*.

D. Jawaharlal Nehru, in his book *'Discovery of India'*, writes on pg. 74-75, that the earliest reference to the word 'Hindu' can be traced to a tantrik of the 8th Century C.E., where it means a people and not a follower of a particular religion. The use of the word 'Hindu' in connection with a particular religion is of late occurrence.

E. In short the word 'Hindu' is a geographical definition or term which is used to refer to people who live beyond the river Indus or in other words to those who live in India.

2.   **Definition of Hinduism.**

A.   Hinduism has been derived from the word Hindu. According to the *New Encyclopedia Britannica* 20:581, Hinduism was a name given in English language in the Nineteenth Century by the English people to the multiplicity of the beliefs and faiths of the people of the Indus land. The British writers in 1830 gave the word Hinduism to be used as the common name for all the beliefs of the people of India excluding the Muslims and Christians.

B.   According to the Hindu Scholars, Hinduism is a misnomer and the religion 'Hinduism' should be either referred to as '*Sanatana Dharma*', which means eternal religion, or as Vedic Dharma, meaning religion of the Vedas. According to Swami Vivekananda, the followers of this religion are referred to as *Vedantists*.

Now we shall examine the articles of faith in Islam and compare them with the tenets of Hinduism as mentioned in the Hindu Scriptures. We shall also study and compare the concept of God in Islam and in Hinduism.

ARTICLES OF FAITH (IMAAN) IN ISLAM & COMPARISON WITH TENETS PRESCRIBED BY HINDU SCRIPTURES

Almighty Allah says in the Glorious Qur'an: Surah Al Baqarah Chapter 2 Verse 177,

> *It is not righteousness*
> *That ye turn your faces*
> *Towards East or West;*
> *But it is righteousness*
> *To believe in Allah*
> *And the Last Day,*
> *And the Angels,*

And the Book,
And the Messengers;

Sahih Muslim Vol. 1 Book of Imaan Chapter 2 Hadith 6.

It is reported in Sahih Muslim :

"... A man came to the Prophet and said 'O Messenger of Allah, what is Imaan (faith)? He (the prophet) said: 'That you affirm your faith in Allah, His Angels, His Books, His Meeting, His Messengers and that you believe in the Resurrection i.e. Hereafter and that you believe in Qadr i.e. destiny."

Thus the six articles of faith of Islam are :

i) Concept of God (The first article of faith in Islam is *'Tawheed'* i.e. belief in the one Unique Eternal Creator of all creation).

ii) His angels

iii) His books

iv) His messengers

v) The Hereafter i.e. Life after death and

vi) *Qadr* i.e. destiny

Let us examine the concept of God in these two major religions in light of their respective scriptures and study if there are similarities.

First we shall discuss the Concept of God in Hinduism.

4

CONCEPT OF GOD IN HINDUISM

If you ask some common persons who are Hindus that how many gods do they believe in, some may say three, some may say thirty three, some may say a thousand, while some may say thirty three crores i.e. 330 million. But if you ask this question to a learned Hindu who is well Versed with the Hindu Scriptures, he will reply that the Hindus should actually believe and worship only one God.

DIFFERENCE BETWEEN ISLAM AND HINDUISM IS THAT OF 'S.

(Everything is 'God's' - Everything is 'God')

The major difference between the Hindu and the Muslim is that while the common Hindu believes in the philosophy of Pantheism, i.e. "everything is God, the Tree is God, the Sun is God, the Moon is God, the Snake is God, the Monkey is God, the Human Being is God", all Muslims believe that "everything is God's '. The Muslims believe that everything is God's i.e. GOD with an apostrophe's'. Everything belongs to the one and only unique eternal God. The tree belongs to God, the sun belongs to God, the moon belongs to God, the snake belongs to God, monkey belongs to God, the human being belongs to God.

Thus the major difference between the Hindus and the Muslims is the apostrophe's'. The Hindu says, "everything is GOD". The Muslim says, "everything is God's", — GOD with an Apostrophe 's'. If we can solve the difference of the Apostrophe 's', the Hindus and the Muslims will be united.

The Glorious Qur'an says in Surah Al Imran Chapter 3 Verse 64,

"Come to common terms as between us and you",
Which is the first term?
"that we worship none but Allah"

So let's come to common terms by analyzing the scriptures of the Hindus and of the Muslims.

UPANISHAD

Upanishads are one of the sacred Scriptures of the Hindus.

i.   Chandogya Upanishad Chapter 6 Section 2 Verse 1

"Ekam Evadvitiyam"
"He is one only without a second."

(The Principal Upanishad by S. Radhakrishnan pg. 447 & 448) (Sacred Books of the East Volume 1, the Upanishads Part I Page 93)

ii. Shwetashvatara Upanishad Chapter 6 Verse 9

"Nacasya kascij janita na cadhipah"
"Of Him there are neither parents nor Lord."

(The Principal Upanishad by S. Radhakrishnan pg. 745) (and in Sacred books of the East volume 15, the Upanishads Part II Page 263)

iii. Shwetashvatara Upanishad Chapter 4 Verse 19

"Na tasya pratima asti"
"There is no likeness of Him".

(The Principal Upanishad by S. Radhakrishnan pg.

736 & 737) (and in Sacred books of the East Volume 15, the Upanishads part II, Page no. 253)

iv.   Shwetashvatara Upanishad Chapter 4 Verse 20

"Na saindrse tisthati rupam asya, na caksusa pasyati kas canainam".

"His form cannot be seen, no one sees Him with the eye".

(The Principal Upanishad by S. Radhakrishnan pg. 737) (And in Sacred books of the East Volume 15, the Upanishad part II, Page no. 253)

BHAGWAD GEETA

The most popular amongst all the Hindu Scriptures is the Bhagwad Geeta.

Bhagwad Geeta mentions 7:20.

"Those whose intelligence has been stolen by material desires worship demigods" that is *"Those who are materialistic, they worship demigods" means —* others as deities besides the True God.

It is mentioned in Bhagwad Gita 10:3

"He who knows Me as the unborn, as the beginningless, as the Supreme Lord of all the worlds..."

YAJUR VEDA

Vedas are the most sacred amongst all the Hindu Scriptures. There are principally 4 Vedas: Rig Ved, Yajur Ved, Sam Ved, and Atharva Ved.

i.   Yajur veda Chapter 32, Verse 3

"na tasya pratima asti"

"There is no image of Him"

It further says, "He is *unborn, He deserves our worship*". (Yajur veda 32:3)

(The Yajur veda by Devi Chand M.A. pg. 377)

ii.   Yajur veda Chapter 40 Verse 8

"He is bodiless and pure".

(Yajur veda Samhita by Ralph I. H. Griffith pg. 538)

iii. Yajur veda Chapter 40 Verse 9

"Andhatma pravishanti ye assambhuti mupaste"

"They enter darkness, those who worship natural things."

E.g. worship of natural elements air, water, fire, Sun, Moon etc.

It further continues and says *"They sink deeper in darkness those who worship sambhuti i.e. created things" E.g. created things such as table, chair, idols, etc.*

(Yajur veda Samhita by Ralph T. H. Griffith pg. 538)

ATHARVA VEDA

i.   Atharva Veda book 20 hymn (Chapter) 58 Verse 3.

"Dev Maha Osi"
"God is Verily Great."

(Atharvaveda Samhita Vol. 2, William Duright Whitney pg. 910)

RIG VEDA

i.   Rig veda Book no. 1, Hymn No. 164, Verse 46

"Ekam sat vipra bahudha vadanti"

"Sages (learned Priests) call one God by many names".

Truth is one, God is one, sages call it by various names. A similar message is given in Rig veda, Book 10, hymn 114, Verse 5.

ii.   Rig veda Book 2 hymn 1

Rig veda gives no less than 33 different attributes to Almighty God. Several of these attributes are mentioned in Rig veda Book 2 hymn 1

a.   **Brahma = Creator = Khaliq : Rig veda Book 2 Hymn 1 Verse 3**

Amongst the various attributes given in Rig veda, one of the beautiful attributes for Almighty God is 'Brahma'. 'Brahma' means *'the Creator'*. If you translate into Arabic it means *'Khaliq'*. Islam does not object to anyone calling Almighty God as 'Khaliq' or 'Creator' or 'Brahma', but if someone says that 'Brahma' i.e. Almighty God has got four heads and on each head is a crown and this Brahma has got four hands, Islam takes strong exception to it because such descriptions give an image to Almighty God. Such descriptions are also against what is propounded in Yajur veda Chapter 32, Verse 3 which says:

"Na tasya pratima asti"
"There is no image of Him".

b.   **Vishnu = Sustainer = Rabb : Rig veda Book 2, Hymn 1, Verse 3**

Another beautiful attribute mentioned in the Rig veda Book 2, Hymn 1, Verse 3 is Vishnu. 'Vishnu' means *'the Sustainer'*. If you translate this word into Arabic it means

'*Rabb*'. Islam has no objection if anyone calls Almighty God as 'Rabb' or 'Sustainer' or 'Vishnu', but if someone says that Vishnu is Almighty God and this Vishnu has four arms, one of the right arms holds the 'chakra' i.e. a discus and one of the left arms holds a 'conch shell' and Vishnu rides on a bird or reclines on a snake couch, then Islam takes strong exception to this, because such descriptions of Vishnu give an image to Almighty God. Such descriptions are also against what is taught in Yajur veda Chapter 40 Verse 8.

iii.   Rig veda Book 8 hymn 1 Verse 1

   "Ma Chidanyadvi Shansata"

   "Do not worship anybody but Him, the Divine One, Praise Him alone"

   (Rig veda Samhiti Vol. IX, pg. 1 & 2 by Swami Satyaprakash Sarasvati & Satyakam Vidhya Lankar)

iv.   Rig veda Book 5 Hymn 81 Verse 1

   "Verily great is the glory of the Divine Creator"

   (Rig veda Samhiti Vol. 6, pg 1802 & 1803 by Swami Satyaprakash Sarasvati & Satyakam Vidhya Lanka)

v.   Rigveda Book no. 6, Hymn 45, Verse 16

   "Ya Eka Ittamushtuhi"
   "Praise Him who is the matchless & alone".
   (Hymns of Rigveda by Ralph T. H. Griffith pg. 648)

BRAHMA SUTRA OF HINDU VEDANTA

The Brahma Sutra of Hindu Vedanta is :

'*Ekam Brahm, devitiya naste neh na naste kinchan*"

"There is only one Creator and no second diety, not at all, never at all, not in the least bit".

All the above quoted Verses and passages from Hindu Scriptures clearly amplify the Oneness and Uniqueness of Almighty God, the Creator of all. Furthermore, they negate the existence of any other deity besides the One, True God. These Verses essentially propound monotheism.

Therefore only if one carefully studies the Hindu Scriptures, will understand and realize the correct concept of God in Hinduism.

5

CONCEPT OF GOD IN ISLAM

The Qur'an too propounds monotheism. So you will find similarities between Hinduism and Islam even in the concept of God.

a. SURAH IKHLAS WITH EXPLANATION

As per Islam, the best and the most concise definition of God is given in Surah Ikhlas of the Glorious Qur'an Chapter 112 Verse 1-4,

> *Say He is Allah,*
> *The One and Only;*
> *Allah, the Eternal, Absolute;*
> *He begets not,*
> *Nor is He begotten;*
> *And there is none*
> *Like unto Him.*

The word 'assamad' means that absolute existence can be attributed only to Allah, while, all other existence being temporal or conditional. It also means that Allah is not dependant on any person or thing but all persons and things are dependent on Him.

It is the touch stone of Theology.

Surah Ikhlas i.e. Chapter 112 of the Glorious Qur'an is the touchstone of Theology. 'Theo' in Greek means God and 'logy' means study. Thus 'Theology' means study of God and Surah Ikhlas is the touchstone of the study of God.

If you want to purchase or sell your gold jewellery, you would first evaluate it. Such an evaluation of gold jewellery is done by a goldsmith with the help of a touchstone. He rubs the gold jewellery on the touch stone and compares its colour with rubbing samples of gold. If it matches with 24 Karat gold he will tell that your jewellery is 24 Karat pure Gold. If it is not high quality pure Gold, he will tell you its value whether 22 Karats, 18 Karats or it may not be gold at all. It may be fake because all that glitters is not gold.

Similarly Surah Ikhlas (Chapter 112 of the Qur'an) is the touchstone of theology, which can verify whether the deity that you worship is a true God or a false God. Thus, Surah Ikhlas is a four line definition of Almighty God according to the Qur'an. If any one claims to be, or is believed to be Almighty God satisfies this four line definition, we *Muslims will readily accept that deity as Allah.* This Chapter of the Glorious Qur'an, Surah Ikhlas, is the acid test. It is the *'Furqan'* or the criterion to judge between the one True God and false claimants to divinity. Hence, whichever deity any human on earth worships, if such a deity fulfills the criteria specified in this Chapter of the Qur'an, then this deity is worthy of worship and is the One True God.

b. ATTRIBUTES OF GOD

To Allah belong the most beautiful names :

(i) The Qur'an mentions in Surah Isra Chapter 17 Verse 110:

> *Say; "Call upon Allah, or*
> *Call upon Rahman;*
> *By whatever name ye call*
> *Upon Him, (it is well):*
> *For to Him belong The Most Beautiful Names*

You can call Allah by any name but that name should be beautiful and should not conjure up a mental picture. There are no less than 99 different attributes to Almighty God. Some of these are Ar-Rahman, Ar-Raheem, Al-Hakeem;—Most Gracious, Most Merciful and All Wise. With many many attributes while, there is one name, crowning one, is "ALLAH". The Qur'an repeats this message that to Allah belong the most beautiful names in:

—Surah Al Aaraf Chapter 7 Verse 180
—Surah Taha Chapter 20 Verse 8
—Surah Al Hashr Chapter 59 Verse 23 & 24

c. NAME ALLAH PREFERED TO THE WORD 'GOD'

The Muslims prefer calling Him (the Almighty) creator (swt) with the Name Allah, instead of the English word 'God'. The Arabic word Allah is pure and unique, unlike the English word God which can be played around with, this can be clarified as:

If you add 's' to God, it becomes 'gods' that is plural of God. Allah is one and singular, there is no plural of Allah. If you add 'dess' to God, it becomes 'goddess' that is a female God. There is nothing like male Allah or female Allah. Allah has no gender. If you add father to God, it becomes 'godfather'. "He is my Godfather" means that "he is my guardian". There is nothing like *Allah Abba* or Allah father in Islam. If you add mother to God it becomes 'godmother', there is nothing like *Allah Ammi* or Allah Mother in·Islam. If you put tin before God, it becomes tin god i.e. a fake God, there is nothing like tin Allah or fake Allah in Islam. Allah is a unique word, which does not conjure up any mental picture nor can it be played around with. Hence, the Muslims prefer the name Allah when referring to the Almighty Creator. But sometimes while speaking to non-Muslims we may have to use the inappropriate word God for Allah.

Allah is mentioned by Name in Hindu Scriptures

The Word **"Allah"**, which refers to Almighty God in Arabic, is also mentioned in

Rig veda Book 2 hymn 1 Verse 11
Rig veda Book 3 hymn 30 Verse 10
Rig veda Book 9 hymn 67 Verse 30
There is an Upanishad by the name ALO Upanishad.

6

SIMILAR VERSES IN ISLAMIC & HINDU SCRIPTURES

We had earlier stated that as per Islam the best and the most concise definition of God is as given in Surah Ikhlas of the Glorious Qur'an Chapter 112 Verse 1 - 4,

Say He Is Allah,
The One and Only;
Allah, the Eternal, Absolute;
He begets not,
Nor is He begotten;
And there is none
Like unto Him.

There are several passages in the Hindu Scriptures, which have the same or similar meaning as of Surah Ikhlas Chapter 112 Verse 1-4,

ISLAM	HINDUISM
Say: *He is Allah, The One and Only.* (Surah Ikhlas Chapter 112 Verse 1)	*"Ekam Evadvitiyam"* *"He is only one without a second."* (Chandogya Upanishad 6:2:1)
Allah, the Eternal, Absolute. He begetteth not, Nor is	*"He who knows Me as the unborn, as the beginningless, as the Supreme*

He begotten; (Surah Ikhlas Chapter 112 Verse 2 & 3)	Lord of all the Worlds." (Bhagvad Gita 10:3) *and "Of Him there is neither parents nor Lord."* (Shwetashvatara Upanishad 6:9)
And there is none Like unto Him. (Surah Ikhlas Chapter 112 Verse 4)	"Na Tasya *pratima asti" "There is no likeness of Him."* (Shwetashvatara Upanishad 4:19 and Yajurveda 32:3)

Remember, the Brahma Sutra of Hindu Vedanta clearly declares:

"Ekam Brahm, devitiya naste neh na naste kinchan"

"There is only one Creator and no second diety, not at all, never at all, not in the least bit".

7

CONCEPT OF ANGELS IN HINDUISM AND ISLAM

We shall now examine the belief in angels of God in these two major religions and study if there are similarities.

1. ANGELS IN ISLAM

Angels are a creation of Allah (swt). They have been created from light *(Nur)* and are normally unseen. They do not have a free will of their own and hence they always obey the commandments of Almighty Allah. Due to the absence of free will they cannot disobey God. Different angels have been appointed by Almighty Allah for different activities. For example, Archangel Gabriel (Jibrail) was appointed to convey the revelation of Allah (swt) to the prophets of Allah.

Since angels are a creation of God, and not God, Muslims do not worship angels.

2. ANGELS IN HINDUISM

There is no particular concept of angels in Hinduism. However Hindus believe that there are certain super - beings, which perform acts, which cannot be done by normal human beings. These super - beings too are worshipped as deities by some Hindus.

8

CONCEPT OF REVELATION IN HINDUISM AND ISLAM

Let us now study what the Hindu and Islamic scriptures state regarding God's revelations or books revealed by God for the guidance of mankind:

i) CONCEPT OF REVELATION IN ISLAM

1. Allah (swt) has sent the revelation in every age. Allah (swt) says in the Qur'an : Surah Raa'd Chapter 13 Verse 38,

"For each period Is a Book (revealed)"

2. Four Revelations mentioned by name in the Qur'an:

There are several revelations sent by Allah (swt) in different ages for the guidance of human beings of the respective ages. Only four revelations are mentioned by name in the Qur'an: these are: Zabur, Tawrait, Injeel and the Qur'an. Zabur is the *Wahi*, the revelation which was revealed to Prophet Dawud (PBUH), Tawrait is the *Wahi*, the revelation which was revealed to Prophet Moses (PBUH), Injeel is the *Wahi*, the revelation which was revealed to Prophet Jesus (PBUH) and The Qur'an is the last and final *Wahi*, the final revelation, which was revealed to the Last and Final Messenger Prophet Muhammad (Peace and blessing of Allah be upon him).

3. All previous revelations were only meant for a particular group of people and for a particular time

and period. Each of the revelations, prior to the revelation of the Glorious Qur'an, was meant only for a particular period and for a particular group of people.

4. The Qur'an was revealed for whole of Humankind Since the Qur'an was the last and final revelation of Almighty Allah, it was revealed not only for the Muslims or the Arabs but it was revealed for whole of Humankind. Further, the Qur'an was not revealed only for the era of the Prophet Muhammad (P.B.U.H.) but it was revealed for the all of Humankind until the Last Day.

a. Allah (swt) says in the Qur'an Surah Ibrahim Chapter 14 Verse 1,

Alif Lam Ra. A Book Which We have revealed Unto thee, in order that Thou mightest lead mankind Out of the depths of darkness Into light -by the leave Of their Lord - to the way Of (Him) the Exalted in Power, Worthy of all Praise!

Since, it was final commandment till the day of judgement, so it was unavoidable to preserve it pure and secured. Hence, it is proclaimed in Glorious Quran : Surah Al-Hijr Chapter 15, verse 9 :

"We have (without doubt) sent down the reminder (the Qur'an) and we will assuredly guard it." (from any violation)

b. Allah (swt) says in the Qur'an Surah Ibrahim Chapter 14 Verse 52,

Here is a Message for mankind;
Let them take warning therefrom,
And let them know that He
Is (no other than) One God:
Let men of understanding
Take heed

c. Allah (swt) says in the Qur'an Surah Baqarah Chapter 2 Verse 185,

> *Ramadan is the (month)*
> *In which was sent down*
> *The Qur'an, as a guide*
> *To mankind, also clear (Signs)*
> *For Guidance and Judgement*
> *(Between right and wrong)*

d. Allah (swt) says in the Qur'an Surah Zumar Chapter 39 Verse 41,

> *Verily We have revealed*
> *The Book to thee*
> *In truth, for (instructing) mankind*

Al Qur'an is God's Word. It is the most sacred scripture of Islam. It is the Last and Final Revelation of Almighty God which was revealed in the sixth century of the English Calendar to the last and final Prophet Muhammad (PBUH).

5. The Qur'an is mentioned in the previous scriptures and in scriptures of other religions It is mentioned in the Qur'an Surah Shuaraa Chapter 26 Verse 196,

> *Without doubt it is (announced)*
> *In the revealed Books*
> *Of former peoples.*

The mention of the Glorious Qur'an, this last and final Revelation of Almighty God, is made in all the previous scriptures and in the scriptures of various religions.

6. *AHADITH* : The other sacred scripture of Islam besides the Qur'an are the *Ahadith* i.e. the sayings and traditions of Prophet Muhammad (PBUH). These *Ahadith* are supplementary to the Glorious Qur'an. While, they did not overrule the teachings of the Qur'an nor do they contradict the Qur'an.

ii) BOOKS OF HINDUISM

There are two kinds of sacred writings in Hinduism: *Sruti* and *Smrti*.

Sruti means that which has been heard, perceived, understood or revealed. It is the oldest and the most sacred of the Hindu's Scriptures. The Sruti is divided into two main parts: the vedas and the *Upanishads* and these two are considered to be of divine origin.

Smrti is not as sacred as the sruti. Yet it is considered to be important and is popular with the Hindus today. Smrti means memory or remembered. This Hindu literature is easier to understand because it speaks about the truths of the Universe through Symbolism and Mythology. The smrti are not considered to be of divine origin but are accepted as human composition. The Smrti lists rules governing the actions of the individual, the community and the society, which regulate and guide individuals in their daily conduct. These are also known as *Dharma Shastra*. Smrtis consist of many writings including the *Puranas* and *Itihaas*.

There are several Holy Scriptures of the Hindus; among them are the Vedas, Upanishads and the Puranas.

1. VEDAS

i)   The word 'Veda' is derived from the Sanskrit word 'vid', which means to know. The word 'Veda' therefore, means *knowledge par excellence* or *sacred wisdom*. There are four principal divisions of the Vedas. (Although according to their number, they amount to 1131 out of which about a dozen are available. According to Maha Bhasya of Patanjali, there are 21 types of Rig Veda, 9 types of Atharva Veda, 101 types of Yajur Veda and 1000 of Sam Veda)

ii) The Rig Veda, the Yajur Veda and the Sam Veda are considered to be more ancient books and are known

27

as 'Trai Viddya' or the 'Triple Sciences'. The Rig Veda is the oldest and has been compiled in three long and different periods of time. The 4th Veda is the Atharva Veda, which is of a later date.

Rig veda is mainly composed of songs of praise.
Yajur veda deals sacrificial formulas.
Sam veda refers to melody.
Atharva veda has a large number of magic formulas.

iii) There is no unanimous opinion regarding the date of compilation or revelation of the four Vedas. According to Swami Dayanand, who was the founder of the Arya Samaj, the Vedas were revealed 1310 millions of years ago and according to other scholars they are not more than 4000 years old.

iv) Similarly there is a difference of opinion regarding the places where these books were revealed and the Rishis to whom these Scriptures were given. In spite of these differences, the Vedas are considered the most authentic of the Hindu Scriptures and the real foundations of the Hindu Dharma.

2. UPANISHADS

i) The word 'Upanishad' is derived from 'Upa' meaning 'near', 'ni' which means 'down' and 'shad' means 'to sit'. Therefore Upanishads means *sitting down near*. Groups of pupils sit near the teacher to learn from him the sacred doctrines.

According to Samkara, Upanishad is derived from the root word 'sad' which means 'to loosen', 'to reach' or 'to destroy', with 'upa' and 'ni' as prefix. Therefore Upanishad means 'Brahma knowledge' by which ignorance is loosened or destroyed.

The number of Upanishads exceeds 200 though the

Indian tradition puts it at 108. There are 10 principal Upanishads however some consider them to be more than 10, while others state that there are 18.

ii) The Vedanta meant originally the Upanishads, though the word is now used for the system of philosophy based on the Upanishad. Literally, Vedanta means the end of the Veda, Vedasya-antah, the conclusion as well as the goal of Vedas. The Upanishads are the concluding portions of the Vedas and chronologically they come at the end of the Vedic period.

iii) Some Pundits consider the Upanishad to be superior to the Vedas.

3. ITIHAS - EPIC

There are two Itihas or epics namely the Ramayana and the Mahabharata.

i) Ramayana is an epic, which deals with the life story of Rama. Most Hindus are aware of the story of the Ramayana.

ii) Mahabharata is another great epic, which speaks about the feud between the cousins: the Pandavas and the Kauravas. It also contains the life story of Krishna. The story of this epic, the Mahabharata, is also commonly known to most Hindus.

4. BHAGVAD GITA

Bhagvad Gita is the most popular and well known amongst all the Hindu scriptures. It is a part of the epic Mahabharata and contains 18 Chapters in Bhishma Parva Chapters 25 to 42. It contains the advice given by Krishna, in the battlefield, to Arjun.

5. PURANAS

Next in order of authenticity are the Puranas, which

are the *most widely read scripture*. The word 'Puranas' means 'ancient'. The Puranas contain the History of the Creation of the Universe, history of the early Aryan Tribes and life stories of the divines and deities of the Hindus. The Puranas are revealed books like the Vedas, which were revealed simultaneously with the Vedas or at sometime close to the revelation of the Vedas. Maharishi Vyasa has divided the Puranas into 18 voluminous parts. Chief among the Puranas is a book known as Bhavishya Purana. It is called so because it gives prophecies of future events. The Hindus consider the Bhavishya Purana to be the word of God. Maharishi Vyasa is considered a mere compiler of the book the real author being God.

6.   OTHER SCRIPTURES

There are several other Hindu Scriptures like Manu Smriti etc.

7.   MOST AUTHENTIC HINDU SCRIPTURES ARE THE VEDAS

Amongst all the Hindu Scriptures; the Vedas are considered the most authentic. No other Hindu Scriptures overrule the Vedas. If there is a contradiction between the Vedas and any other Hindu scripture, the opinion of the Veda will prevail, according to Hindu Scholars.

Thus we have examined and highlighted similarities between the concept of angels and revelation in Islam and in Hinduism as mentioned in their respective scriptures. In subsequent articles in the present series, we shall study the similarities between the concept of prophethood, life after death, fate and destiny and worship in Islam and Hinduism.

Now we shall study the similarities between the concept of prophethood, and the attributes of God, in Islam and Hinduism.

9

CONCEPT OF PROPHETHOOD IN HINDUISM AND ISLAM

A] MESSENGERS IN ISLAM

Messengers or Prophets of Almighty God are persons chosen by Almighty God to communicate His message to the mankind.

MESSENGERS WERE SENT TO EVERY NATION

a. Allah (swt) says in the Qur'an : Surah Yunus Chapter 10 Verse 47,

> *To every people (was sent)*
> *A Messenger: when their Messenger*
> *Comes (before them), the matter*
> *Will be judged between them*
> *With justice, and they*
> *Will not be wronged.*

b. Allah (swt) says in the Qur'an : Surah Nahl Chapter 16 Verse 36,

> *For We assuredly sent*
> *Amongst every people a messenger*
> *(with the command), "Serve*
> *Allah and eschew Evil":*
> *Of the people were some whom*
> *Allah guided, and some*
> *On whom Error became*

> *Inevitably (established). So travel*
> *Through the earth, and see*
> *What was the end of those*
> *Who denied (the Truth).*

c. Allah (swt) says in the Qur'an : Surah Faatir Chapter 35 Verse 24,

> *And there never was*
> *A people, without a warner*
> *Having lived among them*
> *(In the past).*

d. Allah (swt) says in the Qur'an : Surah Raa'd Chapter 13 Verse 7,

> *And to every people a guide.*

SOME PROPHETS ARE MENTIONED BY NAME IN THE QUR'AN AND *AHADITH*

PROPHET ADAM, PROPHET SHETH, PROPHET IDRIS, PROPHET NUH, PROPHET HUD, PROPHET SALIH, PROPHET LUT, PROPHET IBRAHIM, PROPHET ISMAIL, PROPHET ISHAQ, PROPHET YAQUB, PROPHET YUSUF, PROPHET SHUAIB, PROPHET DAWUD, PROPHET SULAIMAN, PROPHET ILYAS, PROPHET AL-YASA (ELISHA), PROPHET MUSA, PROPHET AZIZ (UZAIR OR EZRA), PROPHET AYYUB, PROPHET DHUL-KIFL, PROPHET YUNUS, PROPHET ZAKARIYA, PROPHET YAHYA, PROPHET ISA and last prophet MUHAMMAD (peace be upon them all).

STORIES OF ONLY SOME PROPHETS MENTIONED IN THE QUR'AN

a. It is mentioned in the Qur'an : Surah Nisaa Chapter 4 Verse 164,

> **Of some messengers We have**

> *Already told you the story;*
> *Of others we have not*
> *And to Moses Allah spoke direct.*

b.   It is mentioned in the Qur'an : Surah Gaafir Chapter 40 Verse 78,

> *We did aforetime send*
> *Messengers before you: of them*
> *There are some whose story*
> *We have related to you,*
> *And some whose story*
> *We have not related*
> *To you.*

1,24,000 PROPHETS SENT BY ALLAH

According to a Sahih Hadith in Mishkatul Masaabih Vol. 3 Hadith No. 5737, Ahmad bin Hambal, Vol. 5 page 265-266: *"There were 1,24,000 prophets sent by Allah (swt)."*

PREVIOUS PROPHETS WERE SENT ONLY FOR THEIR PEOPLE

All the prophets that came before Prophet Muhammad (PBUH) were sent for their people and nation, and the complete message they preached was meant only for that time.

PROPHET MUHAMMAD (PBUH) IS THE LAST AND FINAL MESSENGER

It is mentioned in the Qur'an : Surah Al-Ahzab Chapter 33 Verse 40,

> *Muhammad is not*
> *The father of any*
> *Of your men, but (he is)*
> *The Messenger of Allah,*

And the Seal (last) of the Prophets:
And Allah has full knowledge
Of all things.

PROPHET MUHAMMAD (PBUH) SENT FOR WHOLE OF HUMANKIND

a. Since Prophet Muhammad (PBUH) was the last and final messenger of Allah (swt), he was not sent for only Muslims or the Arabs but he was sent for the whole of Humankind. It is mentioned in the Qur'an : Surah Ambiyaa Chapter 21 Verse 107,

> *We sent you not, but*
> *As a mercy for all creatures (worlds)*

b. It is mentioned in the Qur'an : Surah Sabaa Chapter 34 Verse 28,

> *We have not sent you*
> *But as a universal (Messenger)*
> *To men, giving them*
> *Glad tidings, and warning them*
> *(Against sin), but most men*
> *Understand not.*

c. It is mentioned in Sahih Bukhari Vol. 1, Book of Salaah Chapter 56 Hadith 429,

"Allah's Messenger (PBUH) said every prophet used to be sent to his nation only but I have been sent to whole of humankind".

B] AVTARS AND MESSENGERS IN HINDUISM

1. AVATAR ACCORDING TO COMMON HINDUS

a. Common Hindus have the following concept of Avatar. Avatar is the Sanskrit term where 'Av' means 'down' and 'tr' means 'passover'. Thus Avatar means *to descend down* or *to come down*. The meaning of 'Avatar' in the Oxford Dictionary is, *"(In Hindu Mythology) the descent of a deity or released soul to earth in bodily form"*. In simple words, Avatar according to common Hindus means Almighty God coming down to earth in bodily form.

A Common Hindu believes that God Almighty comes down to the earth in some bodily form to protect the religion, to set an example or to set the rules for human beings. There is no reference of Avatars anywhere in the Vedas, the most sacred of the Hindu scriptures i.e. sruti. However it is found in the smrti i.e., the Puranas and the Itihasas.

b. It is mentioned in the most popular and widely read book of Hinduism :

i) Bhagavad Geeta Chapter 4 Verse 7-8:

Whenever there is a decay of righteousness, O Bharata, And a rise of unrighteousness, then I manifest Myself. For the protection of the good, for the destruction of the wicked and for the establishment of righteousness, I am born in every age.

ii) It is mentioned in Bhagawata Purana 9:24:56,

"Whenever there is deterioration in righteousness and waxing of sinfulness, the glorious lord incarnates himself."

2. NO CONCEPT OF AVATAR BUT MESSENGER IN VEDA AND ISLAM

Islam does not believe that Almighty God takes human forms. He chooses a man amongst men and communicates with them on a higher level to deliver his message to the human beings, such individuals are called Messengers of God.

'Avatar', as mentioned earlier, is derived from 'Av' and 'tr', which means to descend down or come down. Some scholars state that God's Avatar indicates a possessive case and actually means the coming of a man *"who is in special relationship with God"*. Mention of such chosen men of God appears in several places in all the four Vedas. Thus if we have to reconcile Bhagavad Gita and Purana with the most authoritative scripture the Vedas, we have to agree that Bhagavad Gita and the Puranas, when they speak about Avatars, they refer to chosen men of God. Islam calls such men Prophets.

10

ATTRIBUTES OF GOD

ANTHROPOMORPHISM

a. GOD NEED NOT TAKE HUMAN FORM TO UNDERSTAND HUMAN BEINGS

Many non - Semitic religions have at some time or the other propounded the belief in the philosophy of anthropomorphism i.e. the concept of God taking human form. Those who believe in it have a seemingly common logic for it. They state that Almighty God is so pure and holy that He is unaware of the hardships, shortcomings, weaknesses, difficulties, feelings, passions, emotions and temptations of human beings. He does not know how a person feels when he or she is hurt or is in trouble. Therefore, in order to set rules of behaviour and conduct for human beings, God came down to earth in the form of a human. On the face of it, this seems to be logical. But we need to examine this.

b. CREATOR PREPARES AN INSTRUCTION MANUAL

Suppose I manufacture a tape recorder, do I have to become a tape recorder to know what is good or bad for the tape recorder? The manufacturer does not have to himself play the role of a tape recorder to understand the stress caused by normal usage or even faulty usage of the tape recorder.

Hence, for the users, as the manufacturer, I write an instruction manual. In this manual I state, "in order to listen to an audio cassette, insert the cassette and press the 'play' button. In order to stop, press the 'stop' button. If you want to fast forward press the 'Fast Forward' button. Do not drop it from a height for it will get damaged. Do not immerse it in water for it will get spoilt". Manufacturers write an instruction manual or a user manual, which contains the do's and don'ts for usage of the machine.

c. **THE GLORIOUS QUR'AN IS THE INSTRUCTION MANUAL FOR HUMAN BEINGS**

In a similar fashion, our Lord and Creator, Allah (swt) does not need to come to earth in the form of a human being to know what is good or bad for the human beings. He, who has created this vast universe, has complete knowledge of His Creation. He only has to reveal the instruction manual for the benefit of humans. Such a manual from the Creator informs and explains: (i) the purpose and objective of the existence of human beings (ii) who created them and (iii) what they should do and what they should refrain and abstain from in order to get eternal success. The last and final instruction manual for human beings from their Creator is the Glorious Qur'an.

d. **ALLAH CHOOSES MESSENGERS**

Allah (swt) does need to come down personally for writing the instruction manual. He chooses a man amongst men to deliver His message and communicates with him at a higher level through His revelations. Such chosen men are called apostles and prophets of God. God conveys His revelations to such persons.

GOD WILL NOT AND DOES NOT TAKE HUMAN FORM

a. GOD CANNOT DO EVERYTHING

Some people may argue that God can do everything, then why can he not take human form? If God ere to take human form, then He would no longer remain God because the qualities of God and the qualities of human beings are different.

i) God is immortal; Human beings are mortal.

God is immortal; human beings are mortal. You cannot have a *'Godman'* i.e. an immortal and mortal being at the same time. It is meaningless. God does not have a beginning. Human beings have a beginning. You cannot have a person, who does not have a beginning and yet at the same time having a beginning. God has no end. Humans have an end. You can't have an entity that has no end and still have an end at the same time. It is meaningless.

ii) God does not require to eat

Almighty God does not require to eat. Human beings need to eat. The Glorious Qur'an says in Surah Anam Chapter 6 Verse 14,

> *And He it is that*
> *Feeds but is not fed.*

iii) God does not require rest and sleep

God does not require rest. Human beings require rest. God does not require sleep. Human beings require sleep. The Glorious Qur'an says in Ayatul Kursi, Surah Baqarah Chapter 2 Verse 225,

> *Allah! There is none worthy of worship*

But He - the Living,
The Self-subsisting, Eternal.
No slumber can seize Him; nor sleep.
His are all things in the heavens and on earth.......

b. WORSHIPPING ANOTHER HUMAN BEING IS AN EVIL

If God takes human form, he would cease to be god and it is useless to worship a human being, e.g. suppose that I am a student of a very intelligent teacher and I regularly take his guidance and help in my studies. If unfortunately, my teacher meets with an accident and has amnesia i.e. an unrepairable loss of memory, it will be foolish of me to yet seek guidance and help in my studies from him. Because this person no longer has the expertise after the transformation of his memory due to the accident. In a similar fashion how can a human being worship and ask for divine help from a god who has given up his divine qualities and has transformed himself into a human being like you and I? If a person can worship a human being then why not others worship you and also worship so many humans around us?

c. HUMAN BEINGS CANNOT BECOME GOD

So an entity cannot be both: God and a human at the same time. For if God retains His divine powers then He is not a human because humans do not have divine powers. And if God were to become a mortal which is a human quality, then he is no longer God, for God is immortal. Later on that same human being cannot become God, because it is not possible for human beings to become God. If it was so, you and I too would become God and attain divine powers.That is the reason why God will never take or rather cannot take human form. The Qur'an speaks against all forms of anthropomorphism. Anthropomorphism is illogical.

d. GOD WILL NOT DO UNGODLY THINGS

Islam does not say that God can do anything. Islam says that God has power over all things. Let us understand this with the help of some examples of matters that God cannot do simply because He is Divine.

(i) God will not tell a lie

God only does Godly things; He does not do ungodly things. God cannot tell a lie. He cannot even have a desire to lie or to make a false statement. God will never, and can never tell a lie because to tell a lie is an ungodly act. The moment God tells a lie, He will cease to be God.

(ii) God will not do any injustice

God cannot do injustice nor can He even harbour a desire to do an unjust act or take an unjust decision. He will not do it and He cannot do so because being unjust is an ungodly act. The Qur'an says in Surah Nisaa Chapter 4 Verse 40,

"Allah is never unjust in the least degree."

The moment God does injustice He ceases to be God. Please realize that God cannot be God and not God at the same time!!! He cannot have divine qualities as a Creator, and yet have the mortal qualities and attributes of His Creation.

(iii) God will not make a mistake

Perfection is a quality only of the Creator. His creation can never ever achieve this quality. We can only try to continually improve and excel but we can never ever be perfect

Hence, can God ever make a mistake? He will never

make a mistake. He cannot make a mistake. To err is human. Making a mistake is an ungodly act. Qur'an says in Surah Taha Chapter 20 Verse 52,

"...My Lord never errs."

Assuming without accepting that God was to commit a mistake, the moment God makes a mistake He ceases to be God.

(iv) God will not forget

God will not forget because forgetting is an ungodly act. Qur'an says in Surah Taha Chapter 20 Verse 52,

"...My Lord never errs, nor forgets."

The moment God forgets he ceases to be god.

e. GOD ONLY DOES GODLY THINGS

(i) Allah has power over all things

The Glorious Qur'an says in several places including : Surah Baqarah Chapter 2 Verse 106;

"for verily Allah has power over all things"

This same statement of Divine Wisdom is emphasized for our understanding:

In Surah Baqarah Chapter 2 Verse 109
In Surah Baqarah Chapter 2 Verse 284
In Surah Al Imran Chapter 3 Verse 29
In Surah Nahl Chapter 16 Verse 77
In Surah Fatir Chapter 35 Verse 1

(ii) Allah is the doer of all, all He intends

The Glorious Qur'an says in Surah Burooj Chapter 85 Verse 16,

"Allah is the doer of all he intends."

And by now I am sure you will yourself admit in all humility and sincerity that God only intends Godly things, not unGodly things.

By ascribing human - like qualities of forgetting, of making mistakes, of getting tired, of needing food, of getting jealous and the like - does one realize that one is mocking God and committing blasphemy by ascribing such attributes to God? Do you think we humans are in any way justified in attributing such human qualities to God? Is it not a better choice, and a truthful one at that, to state that our Creator is free from all such blemishes that ignorant humans ascribe to Him? For the Glorious Qur'an says:

Say : "Allah is free from all such things that they (polytheists) ascribe to Him". Surah Al-Hashr, Chapter 59 Verse 23

Thus we have examined and highlighted similarities between the concept of prophethood, and the attributes of God, in Islam and in Hinduism as mentioned in their respective scriptures. In subsequent articles in the present series, we shall study the similarities between the concept of life after death, fate and destiny and worship in Islam and in Hinduism.

Now we shall study the various prophecies in Hindu scriptures of the advent of Prophet Muhammad (peace and blessings of Allah be upon him).

11

MUHAMMAD (PBUH) PROPHESIED IN HINDU SCRIPTURES

a. Muhammad (PBUH) prophesied in Bhavishya Purana.

   According to Bhavishya Purana in the Prati Sarag Parv III, Khand 3, Adhyay 3, Shalokas 5 to 8,

   "A Malechha (belonging to a foreign country and speaking a foreign language) spiritual teacher will appear with his companions, His name will be Mohammad. Raja (Bhoj) after giving this Maha Dev Arab (of angelic disposition) a bath in the 'panchgavya' and the Ganges water (i.e. purging him of all sins) offered him the presents of his sincere devotion and showing him all reverence said, "I make obeisance to thee, 'O ye! The pride of mankind, the dweller in Arabia, ye have collected a great force to kill the devil and you yourself have been protected from the malechha opponents".

The Prophecy clearly states

i)   The name of the Prophet as Muhammad.

ii) He will belong to Arabia; the Sanskrit word Marusthal means a sandy track of land or a desert.

iii) Special mention is made of the companions of the prophet i.e. the Sahabas. No other Prophet had as many companions as Prophet Muhammad (PBUH).

44

iv)   He is referred as the pride of mankind (Parbatis nath).

The Glorious Qur'an reconfirms in Surah Qalam Chapter 68 Verse 4,

> *"And thou (standest) on an exalted*
> *standard of character"*

and again in Surah Ahzaab Chapter 33 Verse 21,

> *'Ye have indeed, in the Messenger of Allah,*
> *a beautiful pattern (of conduct)'*

v)   He will kill the devil i.e. abolish idol worship and all sorts of vices.

vi)   He (Prophet) will be protected against his enemies.

Some people may argue that Raja Bhoj mentioned in the prophecy lived in the 11th century C.E.i.e. 500 years after the advent of Prophet Muhammad (PBUH) and that he was the descendant of the 10th generation of Raja Shalivahan. These people fail to realize that there was not only one Raja of the name Bhoj. The Egyptian Monarchs were called as Pharaohs and the Roman Kings were known as Caesars. Similarly Indian Rajas were given the title of Bhoj. There were several Raja Bhojs who came before the one in 11th Century C.E.

The Prophet did not physically take a bath in Panch Gavya and the water of Ganges. Since the water of Ganges is considered holy, taking bath in the Ganges is an idiom meaning washing away or making immune from all sorts of sins. Here the prophecy implies that Prophet Muhammad (PBUH) was sinless i.e. 'Maasoom'.

b.   Muhammad (PBUH) prophesied in Bhavishya Purana

According to Bhavishya Purana in the Pratisarag

Parv III, Khand 3, Adhyay 3 Shalokas 10 to 27 Maharishi Vyas has prophesied :

"The Malechha have spoiled the well-known land of the Arabs. Arya Dharma is not to be found in the country. Before also there appeared a misguided fiend whom I had killed; he has now again appeared being sent by a powerful enemy. To show these enemies the right path and to give them guidance the well-known Mohamad (Mohammad) who has been given by me, the epithet of Brahma, is busy in bringing the 'Pishachas' to the right path. O Raja, you need not go to the land of the foolish Pishachas, you will be purified through my kindness even where you are. At night, he of the angelic disposition, the shrewd man, in the guise of apishacha said to Raja Bhoj, O Raja! Your Arya Dharma has been made to prevail over all religions, but according to the commandments of Ishwar Parmatama, I shall enforce the strong creed of the meat eaters. My followers will be men circumcised, without a tail (on his head), keeping beard, creating a revolution announcing Adhan (call for prayer) and will be eating all lawful things. He will eat all sorts of animals except swine. They will not seek purification from the holy shrubs, but will be purified through warfare. On account of their fighting the irreligious nations, they will be known as Musalmaans. I shall be the originator of this religion of the meat-eating nation."

Now we shall study, examine and highlight similarities between the concepts of life after death, and of fate and destiny in Islam and in Hinduism as mentioned in their respective scriptures.

12

CONCEPT OF LIFE AFTER DEATH

IN HINDUISM AND ISLAM

LIFE AFTER DEATH IN HINDUISM

1. **Concept of rebirth in Hinduism - Reincarnation or Transmigration of the Souls**

   Most of the Hindus believe in the cycle of birth, death and rebirth, which is called *'Samsara'*.

   'Samsara' or the doctrine of rebirth is also known as the theory of reincarnation or of transmigration of the soul. This doctrine is considered to be a basic tenet of Hinduism. According to doctrine of rebirth, differences between individuals, even at the time of their birth are due to their past karma i.e. actions done in the past birth. For example if one child is born healthy while another is handicapped or blind, the differences are attributed to their deeds in their previous lives. Those who believe in this theory reason that since all actions may not bear fruit in this life, there has to be another life for facing or reaping the consequences of one's actions.

a) It is mentioned in the Bhagwad Gita 2:22,

   "As a person puts on new garments, giving up old ones, the soul similarly accepts new material bodies, giving up the old and useless."

b) The Doctrine of Rebirth is also described in Brihadaranyaka Upanishad 4:4:3,

"As a Caterpillar which has wriggled to the top of a blade of grass draws itself over to a new blade, so does the soul, after it has put aside its body draws itself over to a new existence."

2. Karma - The law of Cause and Effect

Karma means act, deed, action or activity and refers not only to action undertaken by the body but also to those undertaken by the mind. Karma is actually action and reaction or the law of cause and effect. It is explained by the saying, "As we sow, so shall we reap". A farmer cannot sow wheat and expect rice to grow. Similarly, every good thought, word or deed begets a similar reaction which affects our next life and every unkind thought, harsh word and evil deed comes back to harm us in this life or in the next life.

3. Dharma - Righteous Duties

Dharma means what is right or righteous duties. This includes what is right for the individual, family, the class or caste and also for the universe itself. In order to achieve good karma, life should be lived according to Dharma, otherwise it will result in bad karma. Dharma affects both, the present life and the future as well.

4. Moksha - Liberation from the Cycle of Rebirth

Moksha means liberation from the cycle of rebirth or of 'Samsara'. The ultimate aim of every Hindu is that one day the cycle of rebirth will be over and he will not have to be reborn again. This can only happen if there is no karma to cause an individual to be reborn i.e. it looses its good and bad karma.

5. Rebirth is not mentioned in the Vedas

The important point worth noting is that the doctrine of rebirth is not postulated, propounded nor even mentioned anywhere in what are considered to be the most authentic Hindu scriptures i.e. the Vedas. The Vedas make no mention of the entire concept of transmigration of souls.

6. Punarjanam does not mean cycle of rebirth but means Life after Death

The Common word used for the doctrine of rebirth is 'Punarjanam'. In Sanskrit 'Punar' or 'Puna', means, 'next time' or 'again' and 'Janam' means 'life'. Therefore 'Punarjanam' means 'next life' or 'the life hereafter'. It does not mean coming to life on earth again and again as a living creature.

If one reads many of the references to Punarjanam in Hindu Scriptures besides the Vedas, keeping the life in the hereafter in mind, one gets the concept of the next life but not of rebirths or of life again and again. This is true for several quotations of the Bhagvad Gita and Upanishad which speak of Punarjanam. This concept of repeated births or of cycle of rebirth was developed after the Vedic period. This doctrine was included by humans in subsequent Hindu scriptures including the Upanishad, Bhagvad Gita and the Puranas in a conscious attempt to rationalize and explain the differences between different individuals at birth and the different circumstances in which people find themselves in, with the concept that Almighty God is not unjust. So to say that since God is not unjust the inequalities and differences between people are due to their deeds in their past lives. Islam has a rational answer to this which we shall discuss later InshaAllah.

7. Life after Death in the Vedas

There is reference to life after death in the Vedas. It is mentioned in:

a. Rig veda Book 10 Hymn 16 Verse 4,

"The unborn portion, burn that, AGNI, with thy heat; let thy flame, thy splendour, consume it; with those glorious members which thou hast given him, JATAVEDAS, bear him to the world (of the virtuous)"

The Sanskrit word 'Sukritamu Lokam' means 'the word of the virtuous or region of the pious, referring to the hereafter.

b. Rig veda Book 10 Hymn 16 Verse 5.

"... Putting on (Celestial) life, let the remains (of bodily like) depart: let him, JATAVEDAS be associated with a body."

This Verse too refers to a second life i.e. life after death.

8. Paradise - Swarga in the Vedas

'Swarg' i.e. Paradise, is described in several places in the Vedas including :

a. Atharva Veda Book 4 Hymn 34 Verse 6 (Devichand).

"May all these streams of butter, with their banks of honey, flowing with distilled water, and milk and curds and water reach thee in domestic life enhancing thy pleasure. May thou acquire completely these things strengthening the soul in diverse ways."

Atharva Veda Book 4 Hymn 34 Verse 6 (Ved Pra.).

"Having pools of clarified butter, stocks of sweet honey, and having exhilarating drinks for water, full

of milk and curds, may all these streams flow to us in the world of happiness swelling sweetly. May our lakes full of lotuses be situated near us."

b. It is mentioned in Atharva Veda Book 4 Hymn 34 Verse 2.

"Bereft of physical bodies, pure, cleansed with the wind, brilliant, they go to a brilliant world. The fire does not cause burning in their male organ. In the world of happiness they get plenty of women."

c. It is mentioned in Atharva Veda Book 2 Hymn 34 Verse 5.

"May the realised ones, first of all, take the vital breath under their control from the limbs in which it has been circulating. Go to heaven stay firm with all the parts of your body. Attain the world of light and emancipation, following the path of the enlightened ones (your predecessors)".

d. It is mentioned in Atharava Veda Book 6 Hymn 122 Verse 5.

"O both of you, start to accomplish it, make determined effort to accomplish it. Those having unflinching faith attain this abode of happiness. Whatever ripe offerings you have made in fire of sacrifice, may both, the husband and wife, stand united to guard them with care."

e) It is mentioned in the Rig Veda Book 10 Hymn 95 Verse 18.

"O Aila, the loud sounding clouds, these divines say to you, since you are indeed subject to death, let your progeny propitiate your revered cosmic forces with oblations, then alone you shall rejoice (with me) in heaven".

9.   Hell - 'Nark' in the Vedas

'Nark' or 'Hell' is also described in the Vedas and the Sanskrit word used is 'Narakasthanam'.

It is also mentioned in Rig Veda Book 4 Hymn 5 Verse 4.

"May the bounteous fire divine, consume them with his fiercely glowing sharp jaws like flames, who disregard the commandments and steadfast laws of most venerable and sagacious Lord."

LIFE AFTER DEATH IN ISLAM

1.   Live once in this world and then be resurrected in the Hereafter

It is mentioned in the Qur'an in Surah Baqarah Chapter 2 Verse 28.

"How can ye reject the faith in Allah?
Seeing that ye were without life,
And He gave you life; Then will He cause you to die,
and will He again bring you to life;
And again to Him will ye return."

Islam states that a human being comes into this world only once, and after he dies, he is again resurrected on the day of judgement. Depending on his deeds he will either dwell in heaven i.e. Paradise or he will dwell in hell.

2.   This Life is a test for the hereafter

It is mentioned in the Qur'an in Surah Mulk Chapter 67 Verse 2.

"He who created Death and Life,
that He may try which of you is best in deed;
And He is the exalted in Might, oft-forgiving"

This life that we lead in this world is a test for the hereafter. If we follow the commandments of the Almighty Creator and we pass the test, we shall enter Paradise i.e., which is Eternal Bliss. If we do not follow the commandments of our creator and fail the test then we shall be put into hell.

3. Full Recompense on the Day of Judgement

It is mentioned in the Qur'an Surah Al Imran Chapter 3 Verse 185.

> *"Every soul shall have a test of death.*
> *And only on the Day of Judgment shall*
> *you be paid your full recompense.*
> *Only he who is saved far from the fire*
> *and admitted to the Garden*
> *will have attained the object (of life).*
> *For the life of this world is but goods*
> *and chattels of deception."*

4. Paradise - Al Jannah

a. *Al-Jannah* i.e. paradise is a place of perpetual bliss. In Arabic, *'Jannat'* literally means 'The Garden'. The Qur'an describes paradise in great detail, such as gardens underneath which rivers run. It contains rivers of milk unchanging in flavour and rivers of purified honey. In paradise is fruit of every kind. No fatigue shall be felt in paradise neither shall there be any idle talk. There shall be no cause of sin, difficulty, anxiety, trouble or hardship. Paradise shall thus have peace and bliss.

b. Paradise is described in several Verses of the Qur'an including:

I.   Surah Al Imran Chapter 3 Verse 15

II. Surah Al Imran Chapter 3 Verse 198

III. Surah Al-Nisa Chapter 4 Verse 57

IV. Surah Al Maidah Chapter 5 Verse 119

V. Surah At-Taubah Chapter 9 Verse 72

VI. Surah Al-Hajr Chapter 15 Verses 45-48

VII. Surah Al-Kahf Chapter 18 Verse 31

VIII. Surah Al-Hajj Chapter 22 Verse 23

IX. Surah Al-Fatir Chapter 35 Verses 33-35

X. Surah Yasin Chapter 36 Verses 55-58

XI. Surah Al-Saffat Chapter 37 Verses 41-49

XII. Surah Al-Zukhruf Chapter 43 Verses 68-73

XIII. Surah Al-Dukhan Chapter 44 Verses 51-57

XIV. Surah Muhammad Chapter 47 Verse 15

XV. Surah Al-Tur Chapter 52 Verses 17-24

XVI. Surah Al-Rahman Chapter 55 Verses 46-77

XVII.Surah Al-Waqiah Chapter 56 Verses 11-38

5. Hell – *Jahannam*

Hell is a place of torment where evil-doers undergo the most terrible pain and suffering caused by being burnt by hellfire, a fire whose fuel is men and stones. Further, the Qur'an states that as many times as their skins are burnt, the residents of hell shall be given fresh skin so that they feel the pain. Hell is described in several Verses of the Qur'an including :

Surah Al-Baqarah Chapter 2 Verse 24
Surah Al-Nisa Chapter 4 Verse 56
Surah Ibrahim Chapter 14 Verses 16-17
Surah Al-Hajj Chapter 22 Verses 19-22
Surah Al-Fatir Chapter 35 Verses 36-37

6. Logical Concepts for differences in different Individuals.

In Hinduism, the differences in two individuals at

birth is explained by stating past karma i.e. actions of the previous life, as the cause of the differences. There is no scientific or logical proof or evidence of the cycle of rebirths.

How does Islam explain these differences? The Islamic explanation for these differences in different individual is given in Surah Mulk Chapter 67 Verse 2,

"He who created death and life,
that He may try which of you is best in Deed;
And He is the Exalted in Might; oft-forgiving."

This life that we live is the test for the hereafter.

13

CONCEPT OF FATE AND DESTINY
IN HINDUISM AND ISLAM

1. Concept of Destiny - *Qadr* in Islam

'*Qadr*' is the concept of Destiny. Certain aspects of human life are predestined by our Creator Almighty Allah. For example, where and when will a person be born, the surroundings and conditions in which he will be born, how long will he live and where and when he will die. These are predetermined by the Creator.

2. Concept of Destiny in Hinduism

Concept of Destiny in Hinduism is somewhat similar to that of Islam.

3. Present Conditions are a test

There are several Verses in the Qur'an which clearly specify that our Creator Almighty Allah tests us in several different ways. It is mentioned in the Qur'an: Surah Ankaboot Chapter 29 Verse 2,

> *"Do men think that they will be*
> *left alone on saying, "we believe",*
> *And that they will not be tested?"*

Surah Baqarah Chapter 2 Verse 214.

"Or do ye think that ye shall enter the Garden (of Bliss)

without such (trials) as came to those who passed
away before you?
They encountered suffering and adversity, and were
shaken in spirit that even The Messenger and those
of faith who were with him cried:
"When (will come) the help of Allah?"
Ah! Verily, the help Of Allah is (always) near!"

Surah Ambiyaa Chapter 21 Verse 35,

"Every soul shall have a taste of death And We test
you by evil and by good-by way
of trial - to Us must ye return."

Surah Baqarah Chapter 2 Verse 155,

"Be sure we shall test you with something of fear
and hunger, some loss in goods or lives, or the fruits
(of your toil), but give glad tidings to those who
patiently persevere."

Surah Anfaal Chapter 8 Verse 28,

"And know ye that your possessions
And your progeny, are but a trial
And that it is Allah with whom lies
Your highest reward."

4.   Judgement will be based on the facility provided

Each human being undergoes a test in this world. The test an individual undergoes differs from person to person, depending upon the comforts and the conditions in which Allah puts an individual. He passes His judgement accordingly. For example if a teacher sets a difficult examination paper, the correction is usually lenient. On the other hand if the teacher sets an easy examination paper, the correction is strict.

Similarly some human beings are born in rich families

while some others are born in poor families. Islam instructs every rich Muslim, who has a saving of more than the Nisaab level, i.e. worth of 85 gms of Gold, to give 2.5% of his excess wealth in *Zakat* (Poor Due) every lunar year. This is called the system of *'Zakaah'* in Islam. Some rich persons may be giving the minimum required charity; some may be giving less than what is required while others may not be giving at all. Thus for a rich man, he may get full marks in *Zakat* i.e. charity, some may get less, some may get nil. On the other hand, a poor person who has a saving of less than 85 gms of gold gets full marks in *Zakat*, because he does not have to give this compulsory charity. Any normal human being would like to be rich and not poor. Some may appreciate the rich people and sympathise with the poor, not knowing that the same wealth may take that person to hell if he does not pay *Zakat* and due to this wealth falls prey to temptations of character, while poverty for the poor man may be an easy path to paradise if he follows the other commandments of Almighty God. The converse may be true. A wealthy man may earn paradise by his philanthropy and humility, while a poor person who covets luxuries and hence resorts to unfair means to get them may be in trouble on the Day of Judgement.

5.   **Children born with congenital defects are a test for their parents**

Some children are born healthy while others are born handicapped or with a congenital defect. Irrespective of whether a child is born healthy or handicap, in Islam he is *Masoom* i.e. sinless. There is no question of the child being handicapped due to a carried forward baggage of past sins from 'a previous life'. Such a belief will not inculcate a charitable attitude in others. Others might say that the child deserves his birth defects or the handicap since it is a result of his 'bad karma'.

Islam states that such handicaps are a type of test for the parent whether they are yet thankful towards their Creator or not. Do they retain their patience? Do they continue to persevere?

There is a famous saying that a person was sad because he had no shoes to wear until he saw a person who had no feet.

It is mentioned in the Qur'an Surah Anfaal Chapter 8 Verse 28,

> *"And know ye that your possessions*
> *And your progeny, are but a trial*
> *And that it is Allah with whom lies*
> *Your highest reward."*

Allah (swt) may be testing the parents whether they yet are thankful to their Creator or not. May be the parents are righteous and pious and deserve *Jannah*. If Allah wants to give them a higher place in *Jannah*, He will test them further, e.g. by giving a handicap child. Yet if they are thankful to their Creator, they will deserve a higher reward i.e. the *Jannatul Firdous*.

There is a general rule that the more difficult the test, higher the reward. To pass graduation in Arts and Commerce is relatively easy and if you pass you are called as a graduate without any special title but if you graduate in the field of medicine which is comparatively a much more difficult examination, besides becoming a graduate you are also called as a doctor and the title Dr. is put in front of your name.

In the same way Allah (swt) tests, different people in different ways, some with health, some with disease, some with wealth, some with poverty, some with more intelligence, some with less, and depending upon the facility He gives the individual, He tests accordingly.

Thus the main reason for the differences in the human being is that this life is a test for the hereafter. Life after death is mentioned in the Qur'an as well as the Vedas.

Individual differences are not due to transmigration of souls or 'Samsara'. past sins. These beliefs were added on in subsequent scriptures like the Upanishad, Bhagvad Gita and the Puranas. The repetitive cycle of birth and death, birth and death, was unknown and unheard of in the Vedic period.

Now we shall study, examine and highlight similarities between the concepts of worship and jihad in Hinduism and Islam as mentioned in their respective scriptures. We shall also examine certain similarities in the teachings of the scriptures of Hinduism and Islam.

14

CONCEPT OF WORSHIP
IN HINDUISM AND ISLAM

THE 5 PILLARS OF ISLAM

1. **ISLAMIC CREED**

a. It is mentioned in Sahih Bukhari Vol. 1, Book of Imaan, Chapter 1, Hadith 8,

"Narrated Ibn Umar (R.A.) That Allah's Messenger (PBUH) said: Islam is based on (the following) five principles:

1. To testify that none has the right to be worshipped except Allah and that Muhammad (PBUH) is the slave and messenger of Allah.

2. *Iqamat-as-salaah* (to perform prayers).

3. To pay *Zakaat*.

4. To Observe *Saum* (i.e. fast) during the month of Ramadhaan.

5. To perform *Hajj* (i.e. Pilgrimage to Makkah).

b. **TESTIMONY OF FAITH**

The First Pillar of Islam i.e. to declare, proclaim, testify and to bear witness that no entity or deity is worthy of worship, devotion, obedience and submission except Allah (swt) and to bear witness that Prophet Muhammad (PBUH) is the (last and final) Messenger of Allah. This pillar of faith has already been discussed in the Pillar of *Imaan*.

2. *SALAAH*

a. THE SECOND PILLAR OF ISLAM IS *SALAAH*

Salaah is usually translated in English as prayer. To pray means to beseech or to ask for help. In Salaah we Muslims do not merely ask for help from Almighty Allah but we also praise Him and receive guidance from Him. I personally prefer describing it as programming towards righteousness. To elaborate, consider that during *Salaah*, after Surah Fatiha, an Imaam may recite this Verse from The Glorious Qur'an : Surah Maa'idah Chapter 5 Verse 90,

> *O ye who believe!*
> *Intoxicants and gambling,*
> *(Dedication of) Stones,*
> *And (divination by) arrows,*
> *Are an abomination*
> *Of Satan's handiwork;*
> *Eschew such (abomination),*
> *That you may prosper.*

Allah (swt) guides us, through this Verse of the Qur'an, which is recited bv the Imaam during *Salaah*, that we should not imbibe intoxicants, we should not indulge in gambling, idol worship or fortune telling. All these are Satan's handiwork and we should abstain from these if we wish to prosper.

The English word 'prayer' does not denote the complete meaning of *Salaah* in its full and true sense.

b. PRAYER RESTRAINS YOU FROM SHAMEFUL AND UNJUST DEEDS

It is mentioned in the Qur'an : Surah Ankaboot Chapter 29 Verse 45,

> *Recite what is sent*
> *Of the book by inspiration*
> *To thee, and establish*

> *Regular Prayer: for prayer*
> *Restrains from shameful*
> *And unjust deeds;*
> *And remembrance of Allah*
> *Is the greatest (thing of life)*
> *Without doubt. And Allah knows*
> *The (deeds) that ye do.*

c.   **FIVE TIMES *SALAAH* FOR HEALTHY SOULS**

For a healthy body, human require abo it three meals. In a similar manner for a healthy soul, it is required that we offer *Salaah* a minimum of five times every day.

Our Creator Allah (swt) has prescribed *Salaah* for human beings for a minimum of five times a day in Surah Isra Chapter 17 Verse 78 and in Surah Taha Chapter 20 Verse 130.

d.   **THE PROSTRATION IS THE MOST IMPORTANT PART OF *SALAAH***

The most important part of *Salaah* is the '*Sajdah*' i.e. Prostration.

i.   It is mentioned in the Qur'an :
> *"O Mary! Worship thy lord devoutly,*
> *Prostrate thyself, and bow down (in prayers)*
> *With those who bow down."*
(Al Qur'an : Surah Al Imran Chapter 3 Verse 43)

ii.   *O ye who believe*
> *Bow down, prostrate yourselves,*
> *And adore your Lord; and do good;*
> *That ye may prosper.*
(Al Qur'an : Surah Hajj Chapter 22 Verse 77)

SIMILARITIES WITH HINDUISM

One of the types of Prayers in Hinduism is 'SHASHTANG'

There are various different types of prayers and modes of worship in Hinduism. One of the types is 'shashtang'. The word 'shashtang' is made up of 'Sa' and 'Asht' which means eight and 'Ang' which means 'parts of the body'. Thus, shastang is a mode of worship touching eight parts of the body. The best way a person can do this is like Muslims who prostrate in their *Salaah* touching their forehead, nose, two hands, two knees, and two feet.

Idol Worship is prohibited in Hinduism

i. Idol worship, which is very common amongst the Hindus, is prohibited in Hinduism. It is mentioned in Bhagavad Gita Chapter 7 Verse 20 :

   "Those whose intelligence has been stolen by material desires they worship demigods i.e. idols."

ii. It is mentioned in Svetashvatara Upanishad Chapter 4 Verse 19,

iii. As well as in Yajurved Chapter 32 Verse 3

   "There is no image of Him"

   (Svetashvatara Upanishad 4:19, Yajurved 32:3)

iv. It is also mentioned in Yajurveda Chapter 40 Verse 9

   "They enter darkness those who worship natural things (for e.g. air, water, fire, etc.). They sink deeper in darkness those who worship sambhuti. i.e. created things (for e.g. table, chair, car, idol etc.)".

3. <u>ZAKAT (Poor Due)</u>

a. ZAKAAT MEANS PURIFICATION AND GROWTH

   Zakaat is the third pillar of Islam, which means purification and growth.

b. 2.5% IN CHARITY

   Every rich Muslim who has a saving which is more

than the minimum slab called '*Nisaab*' which is a worth of 85 gms of gold or equivalent, should give 2.5% of his excess wealth in charity every lunar year.

c.   **IF ALL RICH GIVE *ZAKAT*—NO ONE WILL DIE OF HUNGER!!**

If every rich human being gives *Zakaat*, then poverty will be eradicated from this world. There will not be a single human being who will die of hunger.

d.   **ZAKAT ENSURES THAT WEALTH DOES NOT CIRCULATE ONLY AMONGST THE RICH**

One of the reasons for *Zakaat* is mentioned in Surah Al-Hashr Chapter 59 Verse 7,

"In order that the wealth may not (merely)

circulate amongst the wealthy...."

e.   **CHARITY IN HINDUISM**

Charity is also prescribed in Hinduism.

i.   In Rig veda Book 10 hymn 117 Verse 5 (Translation by Ralph Griffith)

"Let the rich satisfy the poor implorer, and bend his eyes upon a longer pathway. Richest come now to one, now to another, and like the wheels of cars are ever rolling."

"If it is expected of every rich man to satisfy the poor implorer; let the rich person have a distant vision (for a rich of today may not remain rich tomorrow). Remember that riches revolve from one man to another, as revolve the wheels of a chariot." (Translation by Satyaprakash Sarasvati & Satyakam Vidhya Lankar) (Rigved 10:117:5)

ii.   Charity has been prescribed in Bhagvad Gita in several places including :

Chapter 17 Verse 20 and
Chapter 16 Verse 3

4. *SAUM* - FASTING

a. DESCRIPTION

'*Saum*' or fasting, is the fourth pillar of Islam. Every healthy adult Muslim is supposed to abstain from eating and drinking, from dawn to sunset, in the complete lunar month of Ramadhaan.

b. FASTING PRESCRIBED FOR SELF RESTRAINT

The reason for fasting has been mentioned in the Qur'an Surah Baqarah Chapter 2 Verse 183,

> *O ye who believe!*
> *Fasting is prescribed to you*
> *As it was prescribed*
> *To those before you,*
> *That ye may (learn) self-restraint.*

Today the psychologists inform us that if a person can control his hunger, it is very likely that he will be able to control most of his desires.

c. FASTING DISCOURAGES ALCOHOLISM, SMOKING AND OTHER ADDICTIONS

Fasting for one complete month is a good opportunity for giving up one's bad habits. If a person can abstain from drinking alcohol, from dawn to sunset, he can very well abstain from alcohol the 24 hours a day. If a person can abstain from smoking, from dawn to sunset, he can very well abstain from smoking from the cradle to the grave.

d. MEDICAL BENEFITS

There are various medical benefits of fasting. Fasting increases the absorption of the intestine; it also decreases the cholesterol level.

e.   FASTING IN HINDUISM

There are different types and methods of fasting in Hinduism. According to Manusmriti Chapter 6 Verse 24, Fasting has been prescribed for a month for purification.

(Manusmriti edited by Dr. R. N. Sharma)
Fasting has also been prescribed in
Manusmriti Chapter 4 Verse 222
Manusmriti Chapter 11 Verse 204

5.   HAJJ - PILGRIMAGE

a.   DESCRIPTION

Hajj is the fifth pillar of Islam. Every adult Muslim who has the means to perform *Hajj* i.e. pilgrimage to the holy city of Makkah should at least perform *Hajj* once in his life time.

b.   Universal Brotherhood

Hajj is a practical example and demonstration of universal brotherhood. The *Hajj* is the largest annual gathering in the world where about 2.5 million people from different parts of the world gather, from U.S.A., from U.K., from Malaysia, from Indonesia, from India and other parts of the world. All pilgrims wear two pieces of unsown cloth, preferably white, such that you cannot differentiate whether a person is rich or poor, king or pauper. People of all races and of all colours gather together in unity to worship the One Creator.

c.   PILGRIMAGE IN HINDUISM

There are various places of pilgrimage in Hinduism. One of the sacred places mentioned in

i.   Rig veda, Book 3 hymn 29 Verse 4 is

"llayspad, which is situated at Nabha prathvi."

'Ila' means God or Allah, and 'spad' means place, therefore Ilayspad means place of God. Nabha means center and prathvi mean earth. Thus this Verse of the Veda prescribes pilgrimage to a place of God situated at the center of the earth.

Sanskrit-English dictionary by M. Monier Williams *(Edition 2002)* states that Ilayspad is "Name of a Tirtha" i.e. place of Pilgrimage - however its detailed location is not mentioned (except as centre of the earth).

ii.   According to the Qur'an in Surah Al Imran Chapter 3 Verse 96,

> *The first House (of worship)*
> *Appointed for men*
> *Was that at Bakka*
> *Full of blessing and of guidance*
> *For all kinds of beings.*

'*Bacca*' is another name for Makkah and we know today that Makkah is situated at the center of the earth.

Later after seven Verses :

iii. Rig veda Book 3 hymn 29 Verse 11

Prophet Muhammad (PBUH) is mentioned as 'Narashansa'.

Thus we can conclude that this Ilayspad, place of pilgrimage mentioned in Rig veda is Makkah.

iv.   Makkah is also mentioned as Ilayspad i.e.Allah's holy place in Rig veda Book 1 hymn 128 Verse 1.

15

CONCEPT OF JIHAD IN ISLAM AND HINDUISM

One of the greatest misconceptions about Islam, not only amongst the non-Muslims but even amongst the Muslims, is that concerning the concept of *Jihad*. Non-Muslims as well as Muslims think that any war fought by any Muslim for whatever purpose, be it good or bad, is *Jihad*.

'*Jihad*' is an Arabic word derived from '*Jahada*', which literarily means to strive or to struggle.

For example, if a student strives to pass in the examination he is doing '*Jahada*'.

In the Islamic context, '*Jihad*' means to strive against one's own evil inclination. It also means to strive to make the society better. It also includes the right to fight in self-defence or to fight in the battlefield against oppression and against aggression.

1.   *JIHAD* IS NOT HOLY WAR

Not only non-Muslim scholars, but even some Muslim scholars mistranslate the word '*Jihad*' as holy war. The Arabic word for '*holy war*' is '*harabum muqaddasah*' and this word is not to be found anywhere in the Qur'an or in *Hadith*. The word 'holy war' was first used to describe the crusades of the Christians who killed thousands of people in the name of Christianity. Today, this term 'holy war' is used to falsely describe *Jihad*, which merely means 'to strive'. In an Islamic context, *Jihad* means 'to strive in the way of Allah for a righteous cause' i.e. *Jihad fi Sabilillah*.

2.   ONLY ONE OF THE SEVERAL FORMS OF *JIHAD* IS FIGHTING AGAINST EVIL

There are different types of *Jihad* i.e., striving. One of the types of striving is fighting in the battlefield against oppression and tyranny.

Many critics of Islam including Arun Shourie quote Surah Al-Tawbah Chapter 9 Verse 5,

"... Fight and slay the Mushrik/Kafir (Hindu) wherever you find them ..."

If you read the Qur'an, this Verse exists but it is quoted out of context by Arun Shourie.

The first few Verses of Surah Tawbah before Verse 5 speak about the peace treaty between the Muslims and Mushriks (polytheists) of Makkah. This peace treaty was unilaterally broken by the Mushriks of Makkah. In Verse no. 5 Allah (swt) gives them an ultimatum to put things straight in four months' time, or else face a declaration of war. It is for the battlefield that Allah says "fight and slay the Mushriks (i.e. the enemies from Makkah) wherever you find them and seize them, beleaguer them, and lie in wait for them in every stratagem of war".

This Verse is revealed and instructs the Muslims to fight in the battlefield and kill the enemy wherever you find them. It is natural, any army general to boost up the morale of the soldiers and to encourage them will say "Don't get scared, fight and kill the enemies, wherever you find them in the battlefield". Arun Shourie in his book 'The World of Fatwas' after quoting Surah Tawbah Chapter 9 Verse 5 jumps to Verse 7. Any logical person will realize that Verse 6 has the reply to his allegation.

Surah Tawbah Chapter 9 Verse 6 says :

*"If any amongst the Mushriks (i.e. the enemies)
ask thee for asylum, grant it to him so that
he may hear the word of Allah and then
escort him to where he can be secure".*

Today the most merciful army general may tell his soldiers to let the enemy go, but Almighty Allah in the Qur'an says if the enemy wants peace do not just let them go but escort them to place of security. Which army general in today's day and age, or rather in the whole of recorded human history is ever known to have given such merciful instructions? Now will someone ask Mr. Arun Shourie why did he deliberately not quote Verse 6?

3. *JIHAD* STRIVING IN THE BHAGWAD GITA

All the major religions encourage their followers to strive in good deeds. It is mentioned in Bhagwad Gita 2:50,

"Therefore strive for Yoga, O Arjuna, which is the art of all work."

4. FIGHTING PRESCRIBED IN THE BHAGAVAD GITA TOO

A] All the major religions of the world have prescribed fighting, at sometime or the other, especially in self-defence or for fighting against oppression.

Mahabharata is an epic and sacred Scripture of the Hindus, which mainly deals with a fight between the cousins, the Pandavas and the Kauravas. In the battlefield Arjun prefers not to fight and be killed rather than having his conscience burdened with the killing of his relatives. At this moment, Krishna advises Arjun in the battlefield and this advice is contained in the Bhagwad Gita. There are several Verses in the Bhagwad Gita where Krishna

71

advises Arjun to fight and kill the enemies even though they are his relatives.

B]   It is mentioned in The Bhagwad Gita Chapter 1 Verse 43-46

(43) *"O Krishna, maintainer of the people, I have heard by disciplic succession that those who destroy family traditions dwell always in hell".*

(44) *"Alas, how strange it is that we are preparing ourselves to commit great sinful acts, driven by the desire to enjoy royal happiness."*

(45) *"I would consider better for the sons of Dhritarashtra to kill me unarmed and unresisting rather than fight with them."*

(46) *"Arjuna, having thus spoken, cast aside his bow and arrow, and sat down on the chariot, his mind, overwhelmed with grief".*

C]   Krishna further replies in Bhagwad Gita Chapter 2 Verse 2, 3

(2)   *"My dear Arjuna, how have these impurities come upon you? They are not at all befitting a man who knows the progressive values of life. They lead not to higher planets but to infamy."*

(3)   *"O son of Partha, do no yield to this degrading impotence. It does not become you. Give up such petty weakness of heart and arise, O chastiser of the enemy!"*

When Arjuna prefers to be killed unarmed and unresisting rather than fight and kill his cousins Kauravas, Krishna replies to Arjun by saying how this impure thought has come to you which prevents you from entering heaven. Give up this degrading impotence and weakness of heart and arise, O defeater of enemy.

D] Krishna further says in Bhagwad Gita Chapter 2 Verse 31-33

(31) *"Considering your specific duty as a Kshatriya, you should know that there is no better engagement for you than fighting on religious principles, so there is no need for hesitation."*

(32) *"O Partha, happy are the Kshatriya to whom such fighting opportunities come unsought, opening for them the door of the heavenly planets".*

(33) *"If however, you do not fight this religious war, then you will certainly incur sin, for neglecting your duties, and thus loose your reputation as a fighter".*

E] There are hundreds of Verses in the Bhagwad Gita alone, which encourage fighting and killing, many times more as compared to such Verses in the Qur'an.

Imagine if someone were to say that the Bhagwad Gita encourages the killing of the family members to attain paradise, without quoting the context - such a deliberate attempt will be devilish. But within the context if I say that for truth and justice fighting against the evil is compulsory, even if it be against your relatives, it makes sense.

I wonder how come the critics of Islam, especially critics amongst the Hindus, point a finger at the Qur'an when it speaks about fighting and killing unjust enemies. The only possibility I can think of is that they themselves have not read their sacred scriptures such as the Bhagwad Gita, Mahabharata and the Vedas.

F] Critics of Islam including Hindu critics speak against

the Qur'an and the Prophet when they say that if you are killed while doing *Jihad* i.e. fighting for the truth, you are promised paradise.

Besides quoting Qur'anic Verses they quote Sahih Bukhari Vol. 4, Book of *Jihad* Chapter no. 2 Hadith No. 46,

"Allah guarantees that He will admit the Mujaahid in His cause to Paradise if he is killed, otherwise he will return him to his home safely with rewards and war booty".

There are various similar Verses in Bhagwad Gita guaranteeing a person paradise if he is killed while fighting. Take the example of Bhagwad Gita Chapter 2 Verse 37,

"O son of Kunti, either you will be killed in the battlefield and attain the heavenly planets (paradise), or you will conquer and enjoy the earthly kingdom, therefore get up and fight with determination".

G] Similarly Rig veda Book No. 1 Hymn 132 Verse 2-6 as well as many other Verses of Hindu Scriptures speak about fighting and killing.

5. Explain Jihad by quoting Scriptures of other Religions

Allah says in the Qur an : Surah Al Imran Chapter 3 Verse 64

> *Say: "O people*
> *Of the Book! Come*
> *To common terms*
> *As between us and you:*

The best way to explain a misconception of Islam is to quote a similar message given in the Scripture of other religions. Whenever I have spoken to Hindus who criticize the concept of Jihad in Islam, the moment I quote similar passages from Mahabharata and Bhagwad Gita, and since they know the outline and the context of the fight in Mahabharata, they immediately agree that if the Qur'an too speaks about a fight between truth and falsehood then they have no objection but rather appreciate the sympathy shown by the Qur'an (Surah Tawbah chapter 9 verse 6).

16

SIMILARITIES BETWEEN QUR'ANIC VERSES AND VEDIC VERSES

There are several Verses in the Vedas which have a meaning similar to that of Qur'anic Verses :

ISLAM	HINDUISM
Praise be to Allah The Cherisher and Sustainer of the Worlds. (Surah Al Fatiha Chapter 1 Verse 2)	*"Verily, Great is the Glory of the Divine Creator."*(Rigved 5:81:1)
Most Gracious, Most Merciful (Surah Al Fatiha Chapter 1 Verse 3)	*"The Bounteous Giver."* (Rigved 3:34:1)
Show us the straight way, The way of those on whom Thou hast bestowed Thy Grace, Those whose (Portion) Is not Wrath, And who go not astray. (Surah Al Fatiha Chapter 1 Verse 6-7)	*"Lead us to the good path and remove the sin that makes us stray and wander."* (Yajur veda 40:16) A similar message is given in Rig veda book 1 hymn 189 Verse 1, 2 (R.V. 1:189:1,2)
Seest thou one Who denies the Judgement (To come)? Then such is the (man) Who repulses the	*"The man with food in store who, when the needy comes in miserable ease begging for bread to eat,*

orphan (With harshness). And encourages not The feeding of the indigent. (Surah Maun Chapter 107 Verse 1-3)	hardens his heart against him even when of old did him service - finds not one to comfort him." (Rıg veda 10:117:2)

SIMILARITIES BETWEEN THE TEACHINGS OF ISLAM AND HINDUISM

1. PROHIBITION OF ALCOHOL

A] It is mentioned in the Qur'an in Surah Maa'idah Chapter 5 Verse 90,

> *O Ye who believe!*
> *Intoxicants and gambling*
> *(Dedication of) stones,*
> *And (divination by) arrows,*
> *Are an abominıtion*
> *Of Satan's handiwork;*
> *Eschew such (abomination),*
> *That ye may prosper.*

B] It is mentioned in :

i. Manu Smriti Chapter 9, Verse 235.

"A priest-killer, a liquor drinker, a thief and a violator of his guru's marriage bed - all of these, and each separately, should be known as men who committed major crime."

Further after two Verses it is mentioned in:

ii. Manu Smriti 9:238,

"These miserable men - whom no one should eat with,

no one should sacrifice for, no one should read to, and no one should marry with-must wander the earth excommunicated from all religions".

iii.   A similar message is repeated in Manu Smriti Chapter 11 Verse 55,

"Killing a priest, drinking liquor, stealing, violating the guru's marriage bed, and associating with those (who commit these acts) are called the major crimes".

iv.   It is mentioned in Manu Smriti Chapter 11 Verse 94,

"For liquor is the defiling dirt excreted from rice, and dirt is said to be evil; therefore a priest, ruler, or commoner should not drink liquor."

C]   Intoxicants/Intoxicating drinks are prohibited in several other Verses of Manu Smriti including

i.   Manu Smriti Chapter 3 Verse 159
ii.   Manu Smriti Chapter 7 Verses 47-50
iii.   Manu Smriti Chapter 9 Verse 225
iv.   Manu Smriti Chapter 11 Verse 151
v.   Manu Smriti Chapter 12 Verse 45
vi.   Rig veda Book 8 hymn 2 Verse 12
vii.   Rig veda Book 8 hymn 21 Verse 14

2.   PROHIBITION OF GAMBLING

As the Glorious Qur'an prohibits gambling in Surah Maa'idah Chapter 5 Verse 90,

O Ye who believe!
Intoxicants and gambling
(Dedication of) stones,
And (divination by) arrows,
Are an abomination
Of Satan's handiwork;

> *Eschew such (abomination),*
> *That ye may prosper.*

a. Gambling is also prohibited in the Hindu Scriptures

Rigveda Book 10 Hymn 34 Verse 3:

"A Gamester/gambler says, 'My wife holds me aloof, my mother hates me'. The wretched man finds none to comfort him."

It is further advised in Rig veda 10:34:13,

"Play not with dice: No, cultivate thy corn land. Enjoy the gain and deem that wealth sufficient".

It is mentioned in Manu Smriti Chapter 7 Verse 50,

"Drinking, gambling, women (not lawfully wedded wives) and hunting, in that order, he should know to be the very worst four in the group of (vices) born of desire".

b. Gambling is also prohibited in several Verses of,

i.   Manu Smriti Chapter 7 Verse 47
ii. Manu Smriti Chapter 9 Verses 221-228
iii. Manu Smriti Chapter 9 Verse 258

CONCLUSION

Inshallah, this research will help mankind to come closer to the Word of the Almighty. This booklet contains just the tip of the iceberg. Some people may require ten signs while some may require hundred signs to be convinced. Some would be unwilling to accept the Truth even after being shown a thousand signs. The Glorious Qur'an condemns such a closed mentality in the following verse of Surah Al Baqarah Chapter 2 Verse 18,

" Deaf, dumb and blind,
They will not return (To the path)."

All praises are for the One and Only Creator Allah, who alone is worthy of devotion, complete submission and worship. I pray that this humble effort is accepted by Allah, to whom I pray for mercy and guidance (*Aameen*).